Original Title: Expression through Dance

Copyright © 2024 Book Fairy Publishing
All rights reserved.

Editors: Theodor Taimla
Autor: Karoliina Kadakas
ISBN 978-9916-748-18-3

Expression through Dance

Karoliina Kadakas

Leap of the Heart

In the silent whisper of the night,
A heart takes a leap, bold and bright.
Through the shadows, it seeks the light,
Yearning for love that feels just right.

Over mountains, vast and steep,
It dares to dream, to love, to leap.
Against the odds, it takes the chance,
In love's sweet melody, it starts to dance.

With every beat, it finds its way,
Through stormy nights and sunny day.
A leap of faith, a hope, a start,
Guided by the rhythm of the heart.

So here it flies, without a chart,
Through uncharted realms, a work of art.
Embracing love's uncertain part,
The bravest journey: A leap of the heart.

The Art of Body Poetry

With a stretch, a bend, a graceful pose,
A story told by the body, elegantly composed.
Silent words flow in kinetic prose,
A tale of strength and beauty, rightfully imposed.

Each movement speaks, a language of its own,
Tales of triumph, of battles overthrown.
In every gesture, a new story shown,
A living canvas, vibrantly grown.

Dancing through life's ebb and flow,
The body whispers secrets, low.
In every step, a new rhythm to know,
A poetic journey, a unique show.

Embraced by the music, in the air it twirls,
Unfolding narratives, as the dance unfurls.
A harmony of being, as the body swirls,
Crafting the art of body poetry, in swirls.

Swaying Towards Serenity

In the calm of the dawning light,
The soul begins its gentle flight.
Swaying towards serenity,
A dance with peace, so tenderly.

With every breath, a step more free,
In the rhythm of tranquility.
Whispers of comfort softly sing,
In the heart, serenity takes wing.

Beneath the vast, embracing sky,
Worries fade, and spirits fly.
Swaying towards a tranquil state,
The soul finds a way to navigate.

In this dance, so serene and slow,
Healing waters begin to flow.
Swaying towards serenity,
In gentle movements, the soul finds harmony.

Tapping into Myself

In the quiet moments, alone, I dwell,
Sifting through emotions, a deep well.
Tapping into myself, I start to find,
The hidden treasures of my mind.

Each thought, a step on a journey deep,
Into my soul, a path so steep.
Tapping into the essence, pure and true,
Discovering parts of me I never knew.

In the reflection of my own gaze,
I find clarity in the maze.
Tapping into strength within,
I gather courage to begin.

With every heartbeat, a newfound force,
A direction set, a steady course.
Tapping into myself, a revelation,
Embracing life with no hesitation.

Unspoken Words on a Wooden Floor

In silent halls where echoes dwell,
Wooden planks keep secrets well.
Footsteps trace, in dust and light,
The tales not told, embraced by night.

Whispers born from creaking boards,
A symphony of unsung chords.
Gentle groans and sighs so deep,
Unveil the promises they keep.

In every scratch, a story hides,
Of loves and losses, changing tides.
Silent sentinels, standing guard,
Harboring tales, both near and far.

Memories in every grain,
Joyous moments, lingering pain.
Unspoken words on a wooden floor,
Echoes of life, forevermore.

Pirouettes of the Unheard

In shadows dance the silent tales,
Whirls of stories, like gusty gales.
Each pirouette, a whispered word,
In the ballet of the unheard.

Tiptoes brush against the floor,
Drawing lines never seen before.
The air listens, the walls perceive,
In every turn, they silently grieve.

Voices soft as a feather's touch,
Speaking volumes, saying much.
With every leap and every twirl,
A quiet voice, in a loud world.

Dances painted in the air,
With the stroke of despair.
Pirouettes of the unheard,
Invisible, yet deeply stirred.

Ballet of the Brave

Upon life's stage, they boldly stand,
In defiance of fate's heavy hand.
Their steps are carved from hope and dreams,
In the ballet of the brave, or so it seems.

With every fall, they rise anew,
Grace in struggle, as strong winds blew.
The courage found in a pirouette,
Tells stories of not giving up yet.

Their leaps, a testament to fight,
Shadows casting off into the light.
A dance of defiance, fierce and free,
Crafting their own destiny to be.

Brave souls in motion, ever true,
An ode to the strength that grew.
In the ballet of the brave they shine,
Each step a verse, profoundly divine.

Gestures That Speak Louder

In the quiet, gestures unfold,
Speaking louder than words told.
A gentle touch, a stern glance,
In every movement, there's a chance.

Hands that write unseen letters,
Embracing souls, breaking fetters.
Eyes that whisper secret tales,
Where words falter, love prevails.

A nod, a smile, a tear that falls,
In silent gestures, love calls.
A language universal, pure,
Transcending words, it endures.

In the realm of unspoken lore,
Gestures convey evermore.
Speaking volumes in the hush,
Love's voice, in a silent rush.

Hushed Heels, Loud Souls

Upon the pavement, heels whisper, hushed,
Soft footfalls in the night, swiftly brushed.
Yet within each step a soul loudly sings,
Tales of silent battles, muted things.

Echoes of dreams, in the quiet, spill,
With each subtle step, a loud heart, still.
In silence, their stories fiercely told,
Hushed heels, loud souls, in darkness, bold.

Amidst the noise, their silence a roar,
Unseen battles, of hopes, dreams, and more.
Each step a verse, in life's grand opus,
Hushed heels, loud souls, moving, zealous.

Steps Sewn with Passion

Each step, a stitch in life's vast tapestry,
Threads of passion, sewn with mastery.
Footprints left on earth's eternal loom,
Moments woven, joy, sorrow, in bloom.

With every stride, a color bright, bold,
A story of courage, silently told.
In the fabric of time, a seamless blend,
Steps sewn with passion, until the end.

A tapestry rich, with dreams interlaced,
Each step, a pattern, beautifully traced.
In life's quilt, each footstep, a precious seam,
Steps sewn with passion, a living dream.

The Soliloquy of a Swing

In the quiet park, a swing gently sways,
A soliloquy of simpler days.
Back and forth, it whispers secrets, old,
Tales of laughter and tears, bravely told.

Empty now, but once cradled dreams, bright,
Under starlit skies, or sun's warm light.
Each push, a hope, each retreat, a sigh,
The swing's song, a silent lullaby.

In its motion, memories dance, untold,
Of youthful hearts, and spirits, bold.
In the hush, its soliloquy swings,
Of life, love, and forgotten things.

Muted Murmurs, Vivid Vibrations

In the quiet, where thoughts loudly resonate,
Muted murmurs, feelings articulate.
A world alive, with vibrant vibrations,
Silent symphonies, of imaginations.

Each heartbeat, a drumbeat, softly spoken,
A rhythm of life, unbroken.
In whispers, the soul's deepest desires,
Muted murmurs, igniting fires.

In silence, a cacophony, unseen,
Vivid vibrations, where dreams convene.
A silent orchestra, playing within,
Muted murmurs, where stories begin.

Fluidity of the Free

Beneath the moon's soft and silvery gleam,
In the night, where quiet rivers flow,
There, my soul swims in an endless dream,
In waters where only the free ones go.

With every tide that rises high and low,
Embraced by waves under starlit sky,
Freedom's current, where wild spirits tow,
In the fluid dance, where seabirds fly.

Upon the ocean, vast, wide, and deep,
My heart sails forth, unbound, untamed, unkept,
In the fluidity where dreams seep,
Across the sea, where the free have wept.

In the gentle sway of the ocean's embrace,
There, my spirit finds its traceless base.

Waltzing in Whispers

In the quietude of a twilight's embrace,
We waltz to the whispers of the wind,
Each step a secret, each move with grace,
In shadows, where light and dark are twinned.

Our silhouettes, entwined, finely pinned,
Moving as if one, in silent speech,
Our rhythm, by the softest breeze, skinned,
In a dance where time cannot reach.

Whispers carry our silent plea,
Through the night, our spirits entwined,
In a waltz that sets the soul free,
In whispers, our destinies aligned.

In the quiet, where whispers weave,
We dance on, in the dreams we believe.

Journeys on Jete

On pointed toes and lifted dreams,
Our bodies soar, defy extremes,
Each jete a journey through the air,
A leap from here to anywhere.

With every spin and every twirl,
Around the stage, our dreams unfurl,
The dance floor, our world, vast and wide,
On journeys, our spirits glide.

Across the boards, we find our flight,
In leaps of faith, through height and light,
Our hearts beat in a dancer's time,
In a rhythm that feels divine.

Through sweat and grace, we tell our tale,
In jumps and turns, we sail and flail,
For in each movement, we find release,
In journeys on jete, we find peace.

The Unchoreographed Truth

In the dance of life, not all steps are known,
We move, we fall, in rhythm of our own,
The unchoreographed truth of our dance,
Speaks of chance, of love, of circumstance.

Without a script, we improvise, create,
In every moment, decide our own fate,
In missteps, in falls, we rise once more,
On this stage of life, it's the will we adore.

We sway in the winds of fortune and trial,
In every tear, in every smile,
The beauty of the dance lies not in perfection,
But in the essence of every direction.

In the chaos, in the unplanned tune,
We dance, we live, beneath sun and moon,
For in the unchoreographed truth we find,
The purest dance of the human mind.

Rhythms of the Soul

In the silent echoes of the night, we tread,
Upon dreams where our deepest fears are wed.
Each step a beat, a rhythm, a rhyme,
In the vast, endless orchestra of time.

Within the heart's secluded chambers deep,
Lies the rhythm that the soul does keep.
A melody woven from strands of fate,
Played on the strings of love and hate.

In every breath, a rhythm found,
In every silence, a profound sound.
Our souls dance to the beats unseen,
In the spaces where words have been.

Through life's tumult and its bliss,
Our inner rhythms never miss.
A symphony of our own making,
In every moment, our souls awakening.

Footsteps Whispered in Motion

Each step upon the earth, a whispered tale,
A journey through time, a ship setting sail.
Footsteps in motion, a silent decree,
Of moments captured, and moments free.

In the hush of dawn, on dew-kissed grass,
Our whispered footsteps together pass.
A language spoken without a word,
In the dance of leaves, their voices heard.

Through the bustling crowd, a silent ballet,
Our steps a story, night and day.
A movement, a gesture, a soft impart,
Footsteps whispered from heart to heart.

Beneath the moon, under starry skies,
Our steps echo the earth's soft cries.
In motion, in silence, together we roam,
Footsteps whispered, leading us home.

Twirling Echoes of Emotion

Round and round, the feelings whirl,
A tapestry of emotion, unfurl.
Each twirl a memory, a moment in time,
A crescendo of passion, a reason, a rhyme.

In the dance of life, we twirl and sway,
Echoes of love, in bright display.
Anger, joy, and sorrow too,
In the dance, each emotion we review.

Twirling in the depths of the heart,
Where shadows linger and dreams start.
The echoes of laughter, tears that fall,
In the twirl, we experience it all.

With every turn, a new echo rings,
Emotions unfold, their stories bring.
In the twirl of life, let passion guide,
The echoes of our souls, side by side.

Heartbeats in Harmony

In the quiet of the night, our hearts do speak,
A language of love, unique and meek.
A steady rhythm, a gentle beat,
In harmony, our souls meet.

Side by side, our pulses race,
In the symphony of time and space.
Every heartbeat, a note played true,
In the melody of me and you.

Through the chaos, through the calm,
Our hearts sing a soothing psalm.
In unison, our rhythms flow,
A testament of love to show.

In the dance of life, through highs and lows,
Our harmonized heartbeats, the love it shows.
Together, in harmony, our hearts entwine,
In the score of life, a love divine.

Whirlwind of the Untold

In the silence of the abyss, whispers stir,
Tales spun in the whirlwind, fervently told.
Each gust holds a secret, tender and pure,
Within the tempest, untold sagas unfold.

Eddies dance with memories of yore,
Carrying dreams that are boldly foretold.
In the chaos, hopes soar and implore,
Seeking solace in the whirlwind's hold.

Amidst the storm, voices gently implore,
Yearning for stories to emerge and mold.
With every twist, ancient truths explore,
The untold magic, boundless and bold.

The whirlwind whispers, forevermore,
In its embrace, countless tales retold.
A saga of whispers, from the core,
In the whirlwind of the untold.

Grooves That Gather Grief

Within the heart's hidden grooves, grief gathers,
Silently seeping through the unseen cracks.
Memories morph into mourning's lathers,
In sorrow's embrace, resilience lacks.

Tears trace the channels, carving them deep,
Pain finds its rhythm, in the solace of night.
Within these grooves, shadowed sorrows seep,
Under the moon's melancholy light.

But even as grief's grooves grow profound,
In their depths, a silent strength is found.
For each tear shed, each sorrowful sound,
Nurtures the heart, where hope is bound.

Grooves that gather grief, in time, heal,
With stories of resilience they reveal.
Embracing sorrow, allows us to feel,
In the grooves of grief, we learn to deal.

Steps Stitched with Stories

Each step we take, stitched with stories untold,
Paths paved with tales of the old and new.
Marked by footprints, bold and beautifully bold,
The earth recalls whispers of the passing through.

Journeys woven into the fabric of time,
Steps heavy with lore, light with laughter's clue.
In every pebble, a story, a climb,
A narrative nurtured by the morning dew.

In the footprints left on sands of lore,
Echoes of past strides resound and imbue.
Histories harbored in the core,
Steps stitched with stories, retold and reviewed.

With each advance, memories amalgamate,
In strides, stories sanctify and celebrate.
Each journey taken, we narrate,
Steps stitched with stories, destinies create.

Motion's Melody

In the universe's vast, echoing hall,
Motion crafts its unique, rhythmical call.
Stars and planets, in dance, enthrall,
Composing the cosmos's grand overture, enthrall.

Every wave, every particle, in tune,
Harmonies in the chaos, a cosmic boon.
Orbits align, under the sun and moon,
In motion's melody, we're all opportune.

Rivers flow with a melody so serene,
Mountains tremor with vibrato, unseen.
The wind hums tunes, where it has been,
Nature's orchestra, endlessly keen.

Life moves to the beat of an unseen drum,
With every heartbeat, with every thrum.
In motion's melody, we find our sum,
In its rhythm, to its call, we succumb.

Silent Stories, Spoken Bodies

In the quiet space where shadows dwell,
Words unspoken, stories to tell.
Two bodies speak without a sound,
A language deep, profoundly profound.

In each glance, a novel unwritten,
Every touch, a verse, smitten.
Silhouettes merging in dim light,
Dancing smoothly through the night.

Whispers of hearts in silent roar,
Conversations on an invisible floor.
Eyes locked in a silent ballet,
Telling tales no words can say.

With every move, a story blooms,
In the silence, true love looms.
Spoken bodies, silent screams,
In this dance, love redeems.

The Ballet of Breath and Bone

Upon the stage of life, they twirl,
Breath and bone, a boy, a girl.
Lives intertwined in dance so fine,
In each step, a line of time.

Muscles tighten, twine, release,
In their movement, a whispered peace.
Beneath the skin, a quiet plea,
In every gesture, a deep sea.

A leap into the unknown air,
Gravity defied with flair.
The ballet of existence, raw,
In every fall, beauty awe.

Bound by rhythm, freed by song,
In their dance, they belong.
Breath and bone in sweet accord,
In their ballet, life restored.

Whispering Limbs in Moonlit Grace

Beneath the moon's ethereal face,
Stand trees with limbs in whispered grace.
Their leaves rustle with tales untold,
In the silver light, secrets unfold.

Gentle breezes stir ancient boughs,
Nature's chorus, to the stars it vows.
The night air filled with a haunting tune,
Played by the light of a silvery moon.

Trees sway with a graceful ease,
Telling stories to the nocturnal breeze.
Each rustle, a verse in the endless dance,
Under starlight, in silent expanse.

In the moonlit night, they stand proud and tall,
Whispering limbs, in moonlight enthral.
The tales of the forest, silently shared,
In the quiet night, mysteries bared.

Echoes of Movement

In the stillness, movement whispers soft,
Echoes of the past, aloft.
Shadows dance on walls, unchained,
In their silence, beauty remained.

Footsteps tread where many have walked,
In their echo, voices talked.
The sway of dance in empty halls,
Echoes of movement, as twilight calls.

The turn of leaves in autumn's dance,
A subtle move, a slight glance.
The world moves in unseen ways,
In its motion, history stays.

Through empty streets and abandoned plains,
The earth moves, its heartbeat remains.
In every echo, a story told,
In movement, life's tales unfold.

Beats Baring Souls

In the rhythm, hearts unfold,
With each beat, a story told.
Souls bared in the pulsing light,
Dancing shadows into the night.

Harmony in every motion,
Emotions deep as the ocean.
Drumbeats echoing desires,
Igniting passion's fiercest fires.

Words unspoken, feelings clear,
In the cadence, we draw near.
Eyes closed, yet seeing more,
In this language, we adore.

Together moving, apart yet close,
In each step, a silent prose.
The rhythm binds, the beat controls,
In this dance, we bare our souls.

Glide, Glance, and Gaze

Glide softly, under the moon's embrace,
Each step a story, a delicate trace.
A glance, a moment, hearts interlace,
In the silence, a timeless grace.

Eyes meet, and the world seems to pause,
In the soft gaze, a whispering cause.
Hands touch, and the universe draws,
Two souls united, without flaws.

Through the night, they dance and sway,
In each look, more than words can say.
The world around them fades away,
In their eyes, the only gateway.

Together they move, in perfect ease,
In their gaze, an eternal peace.
With every glance, they find release,
In this dance, their souls appease.

The Echo of Elegance

In the quiet, elegance whispers,
Softly it moves, like a gentle river.
Its touch, a melody that shivers,
A grace so profound, it makes us quiver.

Through the halls of time, it echoes long,
In its path, beauty and strength belong.
With every movement, a graceful song,
In its presence, nothing feels wrong.

Like a breeze, it passes through,
Leaving a trail of something true.
An essence pure, a hue so blue,
Elegance in everything we do.

It moves in silence, yet speaks volumes,
In its wake, beauty blooms.
An echo that forever resumes,
Elegance, in its endless looms.

Canvas of Choreography

Upon the stage, a canvas bare,
Bodies move with grace, in air.
Each motion paints, a stroke so fine,
In the art of dance, their souls align.

With every leap, a color splashes,
Emotions swirl, in fiery flashes.
The stage alight with vibrant dashes,
In their dance, the moment catches.

A pirouette, a soft, smooth line,
In this moment, their worlds entwine.
A canvas filled with strokes divine,
Choreography, their sacred shrine.

Together they create, a masterpiece,
In every move, a release.
On this canvas, their movements never cease,
In choreography, they find their peace.

Silent Stories in Steps

In silent hallways, footsteps speak,
Echoes of tales from floor to cheek.
Each step a word, a pause a sigh,
Stories unheard, where secrets lie.

Through corridors of time they stride,
Past doors of dreams, where hopes collide.
A silent dance on memory's floor,
Each step a chapter, longing for more.

In the quiet, steps weave a tale,
Of joy and sorrow, of storm and gale.
A journey in silence, yet loud and clear,
Footsteps whisper, for those who hear.

With every footprint, a story's born,
Of silent battles, and hearts torn.
Steps tread lightly, yet leave a mark,
In the fabric of the night, stark.

These silent stories, in steps conveyed,
Unspoken histories, in shadows swayed.
A ballet of echoes, in the night's embrace,
Steps tell tales, in their silent grace.

The Dancer's Silent Voice

With every motion, a silent word,
Her body speaks, though she's unheard.
A tale of passion, of love and loss,
Her dance conveys, no matter the cost.

In the realm of shadows, she finds her light,
Twirling, leaping into the night.
Her silent voice, in the air it weaves,
A story of the heart, in its graceful leaves.

No need for words, her movements tell,
Of battles fought, in which she fell.
And rose again, with graceful might,
Her silent voice, cutting through the night.

Each step, a whisper, a soft caress,
Of inner turmoil, and gentle distress.
The dancer's story, silent yet loud,
In the quiet theater, she stands proud.

Her dance, a language, powerful and pure,
Speaking of emotions, deep and obscure.
In the silence, her story thrives,
The dancer's voice, through her body, arrives.

Shadows Cast by Moving Light

In the dance of shadows, light takes the lead,
Casting figures, a visual creed.
Each movement tells a story, bold and bright,
In the silence, shadows and light unite.

As the flame flickers, shadows grow,
The wall a canvas, for a transient show.
A tale of movement, of shifting sight,
Shadows dance, in the absence of light.

With every shift, a new scene unfolds,
A silent play, as the night beholds.
The fleeting stories, in darkness recite,
In the waltz of shadows, in moving light.

Gentle whispers, the shadows convey,
In the language of night, to the break of day.
A silent dialogue, between dark and bright,
In the ephemeral world, of moving light.

This dance of shades, a silent plea,
In the convergence of light, and shadow's glee.
A spectacle, where silence reigns,
In the ballet of light, where shadow gains.

The Language of Limbs

In the silence, our limbs do speak,
Tales of the brave, and the meek.
In every gesture, a sentence lies,
In every movement, an unspoken prize.

Our bodies converse, in a language pure,
Emotions and thoughts, silently endure.
The subtle shift, a lifted chin,
Speaks volumes of the world within.

With arms wide open, or tightly closed,
Our inner battles, are thus exposed.
The stance we take, the steps we tread,
In the language of limbs, our tales are read.

In the dance of life, each move a word,
A story told, though never heard.
The sway, the leap, the fall, the climb,
Each a verse, in the poem of time.

So let your body speak, let it convey,
The silent stories, day by day.
In the language of limbs, let yourself be,
A narrative of existence, bold and free.

Moving Beyond Words

In silence we stand, worlds apart,
Yet speak in the language of the heart.
Words unspoken, yet understood,
In the silence, our spirits danced.

Eyes locked, a conversation without sound,
Feelings deep, in mystery bound.
In the stillness, our souls whisper soft,
Communicating thoughts aloft.

Moments shared in quiet embrace,
A gentle touch, an upturned face.
Beyond the realm of spoken word,
In the quiet, our hearts are heard.

In the dance of silence, we find,
A connection of the deepest kind.
Words unneeded, when hearts confer,
In the silence, we move beyond what were.

Conversations in Couture

In stitches and seams, stories are told,
The boldness of patterns, in colors so bold.
Fabric whispers secrets of those who dare wear,
Conversations in couture, flair beyond compare.

Each gown, a dialogue of dreams and despair,
A narrative woven with the utmost care.
The tapestry of fashion, where threads intertwine,
Speaking volumes, in design oh so fine.

A whisper of silk, a shout of neon bright,
Clothing speaks louder, in the day and the night.
In the language of fashion, expression finds form,
Conversations in couture, far from the norm.

From the quiet elegance of a simple line,
To the scream of patterns, in a design divine.
Every stitch a word, every hue a tone,
In the world of couture, no thought stands alone.

Elegance of the Emotional

In the depth of our feelings, beauty resides,
Where emotions are oceans, and the heart confides.
Each tear, a verse; each smile, a rhyme,
The elegance of the emotional, surpassing time.

For in the realm of feelings, depth is key,
Expressed in moments, as vast as the sea.
Laughter and sorrow, in harmony blend,
In the elegance of emotions, from start to end.

Through the whispers of joy, and the echoes of pain,
In the warmth of love, and through loss's cold rain.
The spectrum of feelings, so vivid, so real,
In emotional elegance, life truly reveals.

Let the heart speak in colors, bold and bright,
In the darkness of sorrow, or love's radiant light.
The elegance of emotions, in its purest form,
In the tapestry of feelings, we find what's warm.

Rumba of the Rebellious

In the rhythm of resistance, the beat begins to pound,
A dance of the defiant, feet barely touching ground.
Each step a statement, in defiance we twirl,
The Rumba of the Rebellious, a flag unfurled.

In the swirl of the skirts, and the stamp of the feet,
In the dance, we find a retreat.
Against oppression, our bodies sway,
In the rhythm of the rumba, we find our way.

With every move, a challenge thrown,
In our dance, our strength is shown.
Fearless and fierce, in the face of the strife,
The rumba of the rebellious, is the dance of life.

So let the drums beat, let the music play,
In the dance of defiance, we'll have our say.
In the rumba of the rebellious, we take our stand,
Together we dance, hand in hand.

Spin, Soar, Speak

In a vortex of vision, the dancers spin,
Creating whirlwinds where dreams begin.
Each motion a word, each leap a speech,
In the silence, their movements teach.

Soar above the earth, so high,
Beyond the grasp of the mere eye.
With every turn, a story unfolds,
In the dancer's heart, the future holds.

Speak without a voice, loud and clear,
In the language that all can hear.
A pirouette whispers, a jump shouts,
In the language of movement, there are no doubts.

The stage is set, the lights are dim,
In the dance, life and art swim.
Spin, soar, speak, in the endless dance,
In every step, give dreams a chance.

Lyrical Languages of the Limber

With limbs that bend and bodies that sway,
The dancers spell words they cannot say.
In the arc of a back, a sonnet's born,
In the stretch of a leg, a narrative drawn.

Each movement, a verse in a silent ode,
Telling tales that were never told.
The stage their canvas, dancers paint,
Lyrical languages, fluent and quaint.

Their jumps are commas, their falls are dots,
Creating stories, untangling knots.
With every gesture, a new language found,
In the quiet, a loud, profound sound.

So listen closely with your eyes,
And you'll hear melodies in the silent skies.
In the language of the limber, find your voice,
In the dancers' steps, let your soul rejoice.

Timed Tears and Tendu

In the mirror's reflection, a story of time,
Of pain and of glory, of rhythm and rhyme.
Each tendu a struggle, each leap a fight,
In the dancer's world, darkness seeks light.

Tears timed with the music, fall to the ground,
In their silent symphony, the dancers are bound.
Yet, with each drop, strength they find,
In the dance, their sorrows unwind.

The stage whispers secrets, hidden and deep,
Of long-lost loves, of promises to keep.
Each pirouette, a tale of the past,
In the world of dance, shadows are cast.

But as the music fades and the lights grow dim,
The tears dry, and the chances slim.
In the final bow, the end they know,
Yet in their hearts, the dance will forever glow.

The Gliding Diary

A page turns, the curtain rises high,
The dancers glide, as if to fly.
Each step a word, each jump a line,
In this diary, their stories shine.

The stage, a book, the dancers, its prose,
Telling tales of joy and woes.
With every spin, a secret shared,
In their movements, their souls bared.

A pirouette here, a leap there,
In the air, they write with flair.
The audience reads, between the lines,
In the dancers' steps, the truth shines.

As the final act comes to a close,
The diary's secrets are finally exposed.
In the silent applause, the dancers know,
In their gliding diary, their spirits show.

Sculpting the Air with Passionate Precision

With hands that dance in silence unseen,
To mold the breeze, so soft, so keen.
Crafting visions from the wind,
Passions twirl, in air, pinned.

Whispers carried on the gust,
Shapes formed in trust.
Each motion, a stroke of devotion,
Invisible sculptures, full of emotion.

The artist's breath, the sculptor's tool,
In fervent fervor, they do rule.
With each exhale, a form takes shape,
A tender world, from escape.

The unseen beauty, carved so free,
By hands moving with glee.
In air, their art does sway,
Sculpting the void, in passionate display.

Driftwood Ballet: Carving Waves in the Aether

Upon the shore, the driftwood prances,
In the aether, it weaves and dances.
Carving waves, in air so light,
A ballet born from ocean's night.

The wind, a maestro, fierce and grand,
Guides each step, with invisible hand.
Through tempest's roar and breeze's whisper,
The wood's performance makes hearts flitter.

Twirls and leaps upon the beach,
A performance no hand could reach.
Each piece, a dancer in disguise,
Telling tales under the open skies.

With every move, a story blooms,
Of endless seas, and stormy glooms.
Yet in this dance, there lies a peace,
A driftwood's ballet, that never ceases.

The Tango of Tangled Destinies

Two souls in motion, on life's grand floor,
Their destinies tangled, yearning for more.
Each step, a question; each turn, a tale,
Together they dance, through every gale.

In the rhythm of chaos, they find their pace,
An intricate tango, a fervent chase.
With hearts entwined, they move as one,
Under the moon and the burning sun.

Through the crescendo of fate's fierce song,
They glide and weave, where they belong.
In each other's orbit, locked in embrace,
Finding solace in the shared space.

The music swells, a symphony of beats,
In the tangle of life, where destiny meets.
A dance of chance, of hope, of fears,
Together, they waltz through the years.

An Odyssey of Oversteps and Understatements

In whispers soft and shadows deep,
Through journeys long and promises to keep.
A path unfolds with oversteps and sighs,
Where silence speaks and truth belies.

A voyage through the veils of doubt,
Where words are lost, yet meanings shout.
Each step a story, a lesson learned,
In lands where understated turns are spurned.

Amidst the clamor of the unseen fight,
A quiet odyssey into the night.
With subtle gestures and muted cries,
A narrative of love, under sprawling skies.

Through oversteps, a journey wends,
With understated means to unspoken ends.
An odyssey of whispers, of silent roars,
A tale of peace, amidst unseen wars.

Footprints on the Sands of Time

Upon the endless stretch of life's broad shore,
Where waves of time erase the paths we tread,
Each step we take, a tale of moments fled,
Leaving behind the marks of journeys yore.

In silent whispers, our footprints implore,
To be remembered, as forward we're led,
By dreams of tomorrow, by hope we're fed,
Despite knowing all will be washed ashore.

Yet, bravely we walk, in twilight's soft glow,
Crafting with care, each indelible trace,
In sands of time, where our memories flow,
Finding in each a lasting, sacred space.

For in these marks, our essence we endow,
A legacy beyond time's swift erase.

Pirouettes: Silent Screams of Joy

In the quiet hall, under spotlight's beam,
The dancer leaps, twirls in a silent scream,
Each pirouette, a tale of joy, unseen,
A flurry of dreams within a soft gleam.

Silhouette refined, in the air does seam,
Lines of grace and strength, a perfect theme,
In silence, louder than a shouted dream,
A story told in every twirl's extreme.

For in the dance, a joyous scream resounds,
Though not a sound, in the heart it bounds,
With every leap, freedom unconfounds,
The spirit's voice in movement founds.

So let the silent joy in dance be crowned,
Where in every pirouette, bliss is profound.

The Dancer's Soliloquy

In solitude, upon the stage I stand,
The echo of my steps, a soft demand,
A dance unfolds as if by magic's hand,
In every move, my soul's unspoken brand.

With no audience to clap or reprimand,
My shadow's company, on wood and sand,
I pour my heart into the moves I've planned,
A soliloquy no words could ever grand.

Each pirouette, a whisper to the night,
Each leap, a longing for the stars' bright light,
In solitude, my essence takes its flight,
A silent dialogue with passion's height.

So, listen to the steps, the silent plea,
The dancer's soliloquy, a soul set free.

In Every Gesture, a Word

In every gesture, a word unsaid,
Within each movement, stories are spun,
Silent dialogues, in light and shade,
A narrative hidden beneath the sun.

A wave of the hand, a chapter begun,
In the sway of leaves, secrets relayed,
In the dancer's leap, the plot has run,
A poem in motion, gracefully laid.

Each step a sentence, bold and clear,
In the dance of life, we all partake,
With every turn, expressions dear,
In the art of living, our masterpiece make.

So, behold the beauty in each move, awake,
For in every gesture, a world to peer.

Disentangling Dreams on the Dancefloor

In a realm where rhythm reigns, and hearts confess,
Beneath the dim light, our shadows intertwine.
Weaving through whispers of silk and satin dress,
Dreams disentangle, in the dance, they align.

With each step, a story, a pause, a plea,
Hands held, fingers fumble, in search of a tune.
Eyes locked, worlds apart, yet within, we see,
Under the disco ball, our spirits commune.

The beat drops, bounds us in a timeless trance,
Our feet find freedom in this fleeting chance.
A leap, a twirl, under the spell of sound,
On this dancefloor, lost dreams are found.

The Quietude of Quivering Quads

After the run, comes the still, silent sigh,
The quads quake, quietly quivering, shy.
Each step taken, a testament, true,
To the trials, the tracks, the paths we pursue.

Breath heaves heavy, in the hush of the halt,
Muscles murmur memories of each vault.
The quietude cradles, in calm, it clads,
Quivering quads, in tranquility, basks.

A symphony of sighs, the body's soft song,
In the silence, strength and serenity belong.
Though the journey jolts, in joy or in qualms,
In the quietude, there's a quivering calm.

Choreography in the Key of Sea

Beneath the blue, where silence swims,
Creatures curve, in choreography, glide.
In the depth's embrace, light dims,
Dancing in the deep, where secrets hide.

Waves whisper, woeful, in their sweep,
Seascapes sculpt, in the salt, stories sow.
Marine and man, in this ballet, leap,
Enchanted echoes in currents that flow.

A pirouette, a plié, under pressure unmeasured,
The ocean's opera, a treasure, treasured.
In the key of sea, mysteries unfold,
In each movement, a tale, ancient and bold.

Ascending the Stairs of Staccato

Each step, a note, in the symphony of strain,
Ascending the stairs, in staccato, we train.
Breaths breaking, in rhythm, they rise,
Climbing the cadence, under the skies.

Legs lifting, in labor, they lurch,
Every motion, a melody, in the search.
Stairs stretch, steep, in stories untold,
Our ascent, a narrative, bold and bold.

Quivering quads, questing, they quell,
In the dance of despair, where determination dwells.
At the apex, applause, in silence, it sounds,
In the triumph, in tune, where our spirit rebounds.

Odes to the Oceans in Our Veins

Beneath the skin's soft, fragile lace,
Runs the brine of ancient seas,
In every heartbeat, echoes a wave's embrace,
Within us, the deep's quiet pleas.

Our veins, rivers longing for the ocean's grace,
Carry tales of old, whispering with ease,
Salt-kissed breezes, in memories encased,
Our spirits dance, forever to seize.

In us, the tidal pull finds its space,
Guiding through life's vast, unforeseen lees,
With every sorrow, every joy we face,
The oceans in us roar and appease.

From the depths, our truths we trace,
Boundless, enduring, like the seas,
In our veins, their power we embrace,
Odes to the oceans, forever to please.

With a Flicker and a Flare: The Flamenco Spirit

With a flicker and a flare, the dance begins,
Feet tap tales on tired, wooden floors,
Each movement, a whisper of wins,
And losses, and battles, and scores.

Guitars weep, their strings thin,
Voices crack, reaching deep, core to cores,
Emotions raw, worn on skin,
Flamenco, a spirit that roars.

In the dancer's eyes, a fiery twin,
Within their heart, the rhythm soars,
Pain and passion, a seamless spin,
A story told in steps, not in words.

With a flicker and a flare, souls to the wind,
The flamenco spirit, forever implores,
In its embrace, we are all akin,
Bound by the dance, its history adores.

Jazz Hands: The Soul's Clapback

In dim-lit bars, the soul finds its voice,
Saxophones cry, pianos rejoice,
Jazz hands clap, in rhythm, in choice,
A clapback to silence, a definitive noise.

Each note a story, a declaration, poise,
Melodies twist, in air, they hoist,
A dance of shadows, of men, of boys,
In the music, their true selves, they anoint.

Swing beats lead, to the night, they alloy,
Bass lines groove, hips, they employ,
Trumpets shout, in glory, they foil,
In jazz, life's complexities, we simplify, enjoy.

Through improvisation, we explore, we toy,
Jazz hands, the soul's clapback, oh so coy,
In each performance, our worries deploy,
For in jazz, we find comfort, a solace, a joy.

Echoing the Ancestral Beat

In the still of night, drums begin to speak,
Echoing the ancestral beat, a language unique,
Every thump, a tale, of the strong, the meek,
In their rhythm, our heritage, we seek.

Feet stomp, hands clap, spirits leak,
Around fires, our ancestors come to peek,
Through dance, their wisdom, we critique,
In the drum's beat, their voices, not weak.

With every pulse, history's pique,
Tales of battles, of love, of the creek,
In the drumbeat, our pasts converge, oblique,
Guiding us forward, to the future we streak.

Songs woven in the fabric of the mystique,
Drums, a heart, in unison, they freak,
Echoing the ancestors, in cadences antique,
In their rhythm, the strength of the past, we sneak.

Heartbeats in Harmonious Disarray

In the orchestra of our desires, beats askew,
Yet in dissonance, a melody we find.
Each thump, a whisper of what could ensue,
A chaotic symphony, uniquely designed.

In the silence between, our rhythms converse,
A language of pulses, fluent and rare.
Though our cadences might at times seem adverse,
In every mismatch, a perfect pair.

Frenzied beats in a harmonious disarray,
Dancing to a tune only we can construe.
With every skipped beat, to fate we sway,
Our hearts in sync with a love that grew.

In this dissonance, a story untold,
Of heartbeats entwined, a sight to behold.
Every misbeat, a new chapter to unfold,
In harmonious disarray, our future is scrolled.

Unspoken Serenades of the Sole

Silent footfalls on forgotten paths,
Each step a verse, a melody unsung.
In solitude, a soliloquy of wraths,
And joys, on the tip of the tongue.

Beneath the moon's soft, watching gaze,
Feet whisper secrets to the earth below.
Unheard songs of the night's quiet phase,
In every step, a story to bestow.

These unspoken serenades of the sole,
Craft tales unknown to the speaking tongue.
In silence, they play an unwritten role,
A symphony by the night, unsung.

Through the shadowed woods, or streets at dusk,
Each sole serenades in the tranquil hush.
Their tales woven in the air, a fragrance musk,
In every silent stride, a world lush.

Tapestries Woven from Steps

With every step upon the ground,
A story weaves, a thread unwound.
Our paths, like tapestries vast and profound,
In each footfall, a new stitch is found.

From bustling streets to silent hills,
Our steps craft tales, our essence spills.
A tapestry rich with human thrills,
Footprints linger, a memory that fills.

Through cities and forests, in sun or rain,
Each journey adds, a unique strain.
Steps interlock, stories entwain,
A canvas broad, with joy and pain.

Upon this earth, our steps, a dance,
Tapestries woven from chance to chance.
In every stride, a new expanse,
Our footsteps' legacy, a timeless trance.

Between Leap and Landing

In the breathless moment betwixt leap and fall,
The world stands still, a silent call.
Time hesitates, in that space small,
Between leap and landing, we risk it all.

With hearts ablaze, on destiny's wing,
We soar between what loss and love bring.
In that interim, our spirits sing,
Of fears, and dreams unfurling their wing.

The gap between starting and the end,
A journey unseen, around the bend.
Between leap and landing, messages we send,
To fate, a plea, our hopes to mend.

In that suspended, timeless space,
Lies the essence of grace.
Between leap and landing, we embrace,
The infinite possibilities of our chase.

Muse Moves

In twilight's hush, the muse does dance,
Upon the mind, a delicate prance.
Ideas bloom like morning dew,
Each thought a step, a pattern new.

With every swirl, a story's born,
Under the watchful moon, till morn.
Her movements paint the dark with dreams,
Silken threads pull at the seams.

In the quiet, inspiration flows,
As gently as the river goes.
The muse moves, a guiding light,
In creative hearts, through the night.

The Sprinting Spirit

With pounding heart and rushing blood,
The sprint begins, a starting thud.
Legs move with untamed fire,
Every breath a burning pyre.

The finish line, a distant dream,
Yet closer with each stride, it seems.
The world blurs in a race of time,
Each step a note, in life's rhyme.

Victory's sweet whisper calls,
Over hurdles, through the falls.
The sprinting spirit, fierce and wild,
In the race of life, becomes the child.

Rhythmic Revelations

In beats and bars, the truth is told,
In rhythms bold, life's tales unfold.
Each measure a confession made,
In music, our souls parade.

Harmonies hide our deepest fears,
In symphonies, joy appears.
Notes climb and fall like ocean waves,
In sound, our spirit craves.

Melodies craft our inner shrine,
Where words fail, music will define.
Rhythmic revelations, deep and wide,
In every beat, our hearts confide.

Postures of Persuasion

With stance and gaze, the silent words,
Speak louder than can be heard.
In posture's play, intent is shown,
In every gesture, thought is sown.

Confidence strides in open gate,
Doubt slinks in shadows, hesitates.
Victory's pose, bold and bright,
Defeat slumps away from light.

Eyes meet, hearts beat in silent talk,
In every step, a story walks.
Postures of persuasion, subtle art,
In silent language, soul takes part.

Footnotes in the Margins of the Sky

In the canvas vast and ever high,
Where clouds dance and birds fly,
Each star a word, in silence lies,
In the storybook of the night sky.

In the margins wide, where dreams alight,
Footnotes inscribed by the moon's soft light,
Telling tales not spoken, but deeply felt,
In ethereal script, where hearts melt.

With every dawn, the page is turned,
In hues of amber and pink, unconcerned,
The sun pens verses in golden beams,
Footnotes in sky, or so it seems.

As dusk approaches, with gentle sighs,
The sky a parchment, limitless in size,
With footnotes many, in twilight ink,
A moment's pause, for the soul to think.

In the margins of the sky, stories untold,
Of loves and losses, of brave and bold,
In each footnote, a world entire,
Lit by starlight, eternal fire.

Swaying with the Whispers of the Wind

Leaves whisper secrets, in gusts they confide,
To the willows swaying, in the wind they abide,
Each breath of air, a story spun,
Under the watchful eye of the sun.

The meadow listens, to the wind's soft speech,
Tales of far lands, within its breezy reach,
Grasses sway, in rhythmic dance,
With every gust, they leap and prance.

Flowers bend, in the wind's gentle hold,
Their colors bright, their scents bold,
Together in harmony, they sway and bend,
In the whispers of the wind, messages they send.

The river's surface, with ripples wide,
Mirrors the dance, of the wind outside,
The water and air, in conversation deep,
In the language of the wind, secrets they keep.

Swaying with the whispers, of the wind's gentle song,
The world listens closely, where hearts belong,
In each breath, a whisper, a story anew,
In the embrace of the wind, life feels true.

Embracing the Rhythm of the Rain

Raindrops pitter, patter, on the window pane,
A melody sweet, in the refrain,
Each drop a note, in nature's song,
In the rhythm of the rain, where hearts belong.

Streets glisten under the lamp's soft glow,
As rivers on pavements begin to flow,
Every droplet carries a beat,
A symphony felt beneath our feet.

Leaves dance under the rain's tender touch,
In the garden's silence, it means so much,
The petals catch drops, in embrace dear,
The rhythm of the rain, so clear.

The thunder rolls, in the distance it speaks,
A drumbeat fierce, as the sky leaks,
The rhythm intensifies, in the storm's heart,
In nature's orchestra, playing its part.

Embracing the rhythm, in rain's soft arms,
In its tranquil pace, and soothing charms,
Each drop a whisper, of life's embrace,
In the rhythm of the rain, we find our place.

The Unwritten Language of the Heart

In the silence between two heartbeats,
Lies a language, soft and sweet,
Words unspoken, but deeply felt,
In the heart's vast expanse, where love dwells.

Eyes meet, and in that glance,
A thousand words, in silence dance,
No script required, nor spoken part,
In the unwritten language of the heart.

Gestures small, yet meaning vast,
In memories made, and shadows cast,
The touch of hands, or a smile so bright,
Speaks volumes in the quiet night.

In laughter shared, and tears shed,
The heart's true language, silently read,
Beyond words, where feelings start,
In the unwritten language of the heart.

So listen closely, and you might find,
The most profound connections, unrefined,
In every moment, together or apart,
The unwritten language of the heart.

Drifts and Drives of Dancers

In the silent glimmer of the night's embrace,
They move, they glide, in eloquent grace.
Each step, a story, a passionate plea,
In the drifts and drives, they're wild and free.

Through shadows, they whisper, in light, they roar,
With each turn, their spirits soar.
Their dance, a battle, a lover's embrace,
In the drifts and drives, they find their place.

Limbs stretching far, as if to claim,
The world's stage, their rightful domain.
In the silence, their movements scream,
In the drifts and drives, they dream.

With the rhythm, they bend, with grace, they fly,
Under the watchful gaze of the moonlit sky.
The night's melody, their steadfast guide,
In the drifts and drives, they bravely stride.

Their shadows, a dance of fleeting sighs,
Echo the tales of ancient ties.
In the drifts and drives, with every move,
They narrate the stories they yearn to prove.

Pathways Paved in Pirouettes

On pathways paved with dreams and pirouettes,
Dancers twirl, their silhouettes aglow.
Each spin weaves stories, no words can tell,
In ballets of breath, where emotions flow.

Through leaps and bounds, they chase the wind,
Their hearts in sync with the earth's spin.
With every pirouette, a new world unfurls,
Capturing the essence of the untold whirls.

In the mirror of the stage, reflections dance,
Twisting and turning in a hypnotic trance.
Pathways paved in the daring of their dives,
Where freedom and rhythm harmoniously thrives.

The grace of a foot, the whisper of a turn,
In their motion, a fervent passion burns.
Through pirouettes, their pathways are paved,
In the art of the dance, they are bravely saved.

To the beat of the heart, their steps ring true,
On this canvas of air, their spirits flew.
In every gesture, a universe expands,
On pathways paved in pirouettes, they stand.

Hymns of the Hips

In the rhythm of the night, hips sway,
Singing hymns of ancient pathways.
The beat, a drum, deep and profound,
In the curve of motion, secrets are found.

With each sway, a story unfolds,
Of distant lands and tales untold.
Hips moving in harmonious rhyme,
Keeping the tempo, beating time.

The dance floor, their sacred ground,
Where the hymns of the hips resound.
With every movement, a prayer is cast,
In this moment, free at last.

The language of the body speaks loud,
In the crowd, their dance is proud.
Through the hymns of the hips, they find,
The connection of the soul and mind.

Let the music take you, let it slip,
Into the sacred dance, the rhythmic trip.
The hymns of the hips, a celestial gift,
In their sway, the world will shift.

Telling Tales with Toes

Telling tales with toes upon the floor,
Each step, a chapter, in folklore.
With pointed grace, they sketch the air,
In dancing scripts, they lay their stories bare.

In silent whispers, toes converse,
With the ground, their tales immerse.
A leap, a land, a gentle glide,
In these movements, their stories confide.

The stage, a book, their feet, the pen,
Writing epics beyond our ken.
Through pirouette, through jeté, they soar,
Telling tales of triumph, of lore.

With every touch, a rhythm born,
From twilight's break to the blush of dawn.
Toes tapping in a spirited spree,
In their dance, life's narratives flee.

So, watch them move, hear what they say,
The tales they tell, in their ballet.
With every step, a word, a prose,
In telling tales, with toes, they compose.

Momentum: The Language of the Limbs

In haste, the limbs speak volumes, unspoken,
Their flurry casting tales in the air.
Each movement, a word, a gesture, a token,
Of the stories our bodies dare to share.

With every leap, a narrative unfolds,
In the physics of our ceaseless dance.
A harmony of motion, gracefully bold,
A testament to time's fleeting glance.

The limbs articulate with precision,
A dialect born from the heart's rhythm.
In their sway lies a silent decision,
To convey life's most vibrant algorithm.

This language, universal, intimate,
Tells of struggles, triumphs, the intrinsic.
A silent orchestra, so articulate,
In momentum, the body's linguistic.

Through the tempo of our existence swift,
The limbs chant in unison, wide and sift,
In the dance of life, a most precious gift,
Their stories, in momentum, a drift.

Twisting Narratives: A Body's Tale

With every twist, a story bends,
In the fibers of our forms.
Each gesture shifts, narrative sends,
A message as a storm.

Bones whisper secrets, muscles shout,
In the library of the skin.
A tale of strength, of fear, of doubt,
Of every place we've been.

The archives in our posture hold,
Histories untold, reborn.
In every bend, a mystery unfolds,
From the very moment we were born.

A body's tale, complex, profound,
In every motion, a verse.
A narrative twisting, unbound,
In our corporeal universe.

Sculpted by time, etched by fate,
The body speaks, twists narrate,
Through every gesture articulate,
In our flesh, stories resonate.

Unfurling the Petals of Performance

On stages set beneath the vast sky's gaze,
Performers bloom, their essence on display.
Like petals unfurling at dawn's first rays,
They captivate, in vibrant disarray.

Each motion crafts the petal's tender curve,
The artistry in flutters, leaps, and sways.
Emotions traced in arcs they bravely serve,
A blooming testament to passion's blaze.

In every gesture, beauty's truth revealed,
A flowering of soul, of heart, of mind.
In performance, the inner light unsealed,
A blossoming for all of humankind.

With every note, the petals spread wide,
The dancers' fervor, impossible to hide,
In this unfurling, we all reside,
In art's embrace, we are unified.

Through performance, our spirits merge and meet,
As petals open, our hearts beat,
In every unfolding, bitter and sweet,
In the dance of life, we are complete.

Shadows Dancing in the Absence of Light

In the absence of light, shadows play,
The silent music of the unseen day.
They dance on walls, in whispers they say,
Of the world that exists in grey.

Ghosts of movement, fleeting and shy,
Tell tales in the corner of our eye.
A ballet of darkness, under the sky,
Where the essence of absence draws nigh.

Yet in this dance, a beauty profound,
In the spaces where light is not found.
Shadows twirl, without a sound,
In their silence, our thoughts are unbound.

A spectral waltz, both eerie and grand,
In the gloom, a mysterious land.
With each movement, a story expands,
In the dance of shadows, we understand.

In the absence of light, forms align,
Shadows dance, in darkness, they shine,
A paradox of the night, bittersweet, divine,
In their silent ballet, the world redefines.

The Ephemeral Eloquence of Steps

In whispered winds, where steps converge,
Our tales unfold, then swiftly surge.
Each print, a word; each stride, a verse,
In life's grand book, briefly immerse.

Time's fleeting dance, through hours laced,
In every step, a story traced.
Gone with the dawn, like dew's embrace,
Yet in the heart, they find their place.

With silent speech, steps do declare,
A journey's worth, laid bare, yet rare.
Through paths untold, with care, we tread,
In steps, our fleeting tales are read.

In every walk, a whisper heard,
A fleeting touch, the soul is stirred.
The eloquence of steps, a gift,
In moments swift, our spirits lift.

Embodied Verses, Etched in Air

Our bodies move, in silence speak,
Emotions strong, yet manner meek.
Each motion a verse, in air inscribed,
Upon the void, our tales described.

With every gesture, feelings bloom,
Invisible ink fills the room.
An artist's brush, the body sways,
Embodies verses, in subtle ways.

A language rich, beyond the word,
In movement's grace, our stories heard.
Through dances wild, or gestures slight,
In every motion, our souls alight.

Ephemeral art, in space defined,
By body's curve, emotion's line.
The air our canvas, vast and clear,
Our embodied verses, cherished dear.

A Symphony of Gestures

In silence, gestures weave a tune,
A symphony that hums by noon.
With every nod, a note is played,
In sway of hands, a melody made.

A conductor's baton, the body leads,
Through unspoken notes, the spirit feeds.
The orchestra of life, diverse in form,
In gestures small, emotions warm.

Each movement, a chord struck deep,
In the heart's vast chamber, secrets keep.
A language universal, yet understood,
By those who listen, beneath the wood.

With eyes closed tightly, still we hear,
This symphony of gestures, loud and clear.
The music of mankind, in action found,
In every gesture, life's pulse is bound.

Canvas of the Cosmos: Dances of the Divine

Upon the cosmic canvas vast,
Stars twirl, in dances cast.
Galaxies in pirouettes align,
Universes sway, in designs divine.

Each nebula, a brush of light,
Paints the dark in colors bright.
Through endless black, they gracefully spin,
A celestial ballet, woven thin.

Planets orbit in majestic grace,
In the cosmos' embrace, they trace.
A path choreographed by unseen hands,
In this grand stage, the divine stands.

In the quiet of the night so still,
The universe dances, at its own will.
A performance eternal, on canvas wide,
In every star's twirl, the divine reside.

Cadence of the Concealed

In shadows deep, where whispers dwell,
Beneath the cloak of night's embrace,
Secrets stir, with tales to tell,
In the hushed cadence of this place.

Within the heart, concealed desires,
Smolder in silence, unseen, unheard,
The gentle beat of covert fires,
In every unspoken word.

Through veils of mystery, they thread,
With steps as soft as falling snow,
In the realm of the unsaid,
Where only the concealed dare go.

Echoes of thoughts, subtly interwoven,
In the tapestry of the mind,
Whispers of the heart, softly spoken,
In the cadence of the concealed, you find.

Twists Telling Tales

In the labyrinth of life, where pathways twist and turn,
Stories are born, in the corners where shadows lie,
Every twist and tale, a lesson to learn,
Under the vast, ever-changing sky.

With each bend, a new narrative unfolds,
Eclipsing what was known with what's now told,
In the twists, stories of old and new are woven,
In the fabric of time, endlessly cloven.

Where twists tell tales of loves lost and found,
Of dreams chased, in the playground of fate,
In the silence, there's a profound sound,
Of destiny calling, neither early nor late.

And so we move, through twists and tales,
With hearts exposed like leaves to gales,
In every turn, life's mystery prevails,
In tales that twist, truth never fails.

Harmony in Heel and Toe

In the dance of life, where heel meets toe,
A rhythm emerges, steady and slow,
Each step, a note in the melody of being,
In the movement, a harmony worth seeing.

With grace and poise, under the moon's glow,
In heel and toe, the dancers flow,
Their silhouettes painting the night's air,
A tale of synchrony, uniquely rare.

In every turn, a whisper of joy,
In every leap, a world to deploy,
In the dance, a universe reborn,
From dusk's first light to the break of dawn.

So let the music guide your feet,
In heel and toe, let heartbeats meet,
The harmony found in a dancer's leap,
In life's grand dance, a rhythm to keep.

Patterns of the Passionate

In the heart of the fervent, a pattern lies,
A tapestry of desire, under the skies,
Each thread, a pulse of relentless dreams,
In the weave of passion, a radiant beam.

Through the fabric of fervor, colors dance,
In every hue, a chance for romance,
The patterns of the passionate, bold and bright,
In the darkest of nights, they are the light.

In the swirl of emotions, intense and deep,
In the patterns, sacred promises keep,
Where love and longing harmoniously blend,
In passionate patterns, without end.

Each stitch a testament to the fire within,
In the weave of desire, where dreams begin,
The passionate's pattern, intricate and free,
In the tapestry of love, forever to be.

Vibrations of a Veiled Heart

Beneath a shroud of silence, beats concealed,
A heart whose whispers, subtly revealed,
Through vibrations soft, yet fervently felt,
Secrets and desires, in darkness, melt.

Veiled beneath the cloak of night's embrace,
Its rhythm dances, a delicate trace,
The echoes of which, in the void, confide,
Murmurs of love, where secrets reside.

In every beat, a story untold,
Of passions warm, and sorrows cold,
A symphony played on silent strings,
A veiled heart, and the song it sings.

Through the shield, its essence bleeds,
A dulcet tune the spirit heeds,
In every throb, life's mysteries part,
The quiet pulses of a veiled heart.

Kinetic Conversations

In motion, our truths find their speech,
Body to body, their language we teach,
In the dance of shadows, in the light's play,
Silent words, loud as day.

Limbs articulate with precision keen,
Telling tales, unseen yet seen,
Each movement a sentence, a gesture a word,
A dialogue without sound is heard.

Eyes locked in silent debate,
Emotions swirl, love and hate,
In the kinetic exchange, no lies,
Only the truth in physical replies.

Hands touch, the air crackles, alive,
In their dance, only the genuine thrive,
In the realm of motion, conversations flow,
Where words halt, movements grow.

Our bodies converse, in space, unfold,
Stories ancient, and tales untold,
In each step, a paragraph, in each turn, a rhyme,
Kinetic conversations, transcending time.

Flow of the Unfettered

In the stream of the fearless, waters rush,
Past the banks of doubt, in a silent hush,
Unbound, unchained, their essence pure,
In their clarity, courage, and allure.

Through the valleys of the unfazed, they roam,
Over stones unturned, in their frothy foam,
No dams to hold, no fences to tether,
In their might, they weave nature's feather.

In each ripple, a story of defiance,
In every wave, a testament to reliance,
With each surge, they sculpt the earth,
Carving paths of relentless mirth.

Beneath the moon, under the sun's glare,
The waters whisper, in the air,
A melody of freedom, a hymn so sweet,
The flow of the unfettered, never to retreat.

Their journey endless, spirit wild,
Nature's untamed, unspoiled child,
In their wake, life blossoms, spread,
The flow of the unfettered, forever ahead.

Balletic Breaths

In the quietude of dawn's first light,
Breaths rise and fall, in balletic flight,
Each inhale a lift, each exhale a bow,
In the rhythm of life, a silent vow.

With grace, they twirl, in the air so clear,
In the auditorium of day, they appear,
No audience to watch, no applause to heed,
Just the dance of breath, in its tranquil creed.

In every movement, a harmony found,
In the space between, a sacred ground,
With every rise, a stretch to the skies,
With every fall, a contented sigh.

The ballet unfolds, with the day's embrace,
In the light, their shadows trace,
A silent performance, so profound,
In each breath, life's rhythm is found.

As day turns to night, and shadows grow long,
The balletic breaths continue their song,
In the silence of stars, under the moon's watch,
In their gentle dance, peace and serenity botch.

Gliding on the Edge of Dreams

In the quiet night, under starlight beams,
Gliding on the edge, so seamless it seems.
Where the sky meets thought, in a silken seam,
Dreamers dance, their hopes in gentle streams.

In the realm of sleep, where the lost are found,
Sorrows swim away, in the silence, drowned.
With each breath inhaled, peace is tightly wound,
In dreams, we glide, with no boundary, no bound.

Whispers of the night, tell tales untold,
Of heroes brave and knights so bold.
In dreams, their adventures unfold,
In stories of love, loss, and gold.

Upon the edge, where reality frays,
Dreamers stand, in the twilight haze.
With each step, their fears ablaze,
Yet they dance on, in the moon's soft gaze.

In the embrace of night, we find release,
From the chains of day, a moment's peace.
On the edge of dreams, our spirits increase,
In the quiet, our heartbeats cease.

Transcending Silence with a Spin

In the void of quiet, where thoughts begin,
A spin transcends silence, a delicate din.
With each pirouette, a new world spins within,
In the dance of life, we silently grin.

Words unspoken, in motion, find voice,
In the whirl of shadows, we make our choice.
Silent screams, in gestures, rejoice,
In the dance, our souls find poise.

With each turn, a story silently told,
Of bonds that glitter, brighter than gold.
In silence, our deepest fears unfold,
Yet in the dance, we remain bold.

In the silence, our spirits entwine,
Through the spin, our fates align.
In movements, our hopes define,
Beyond words, our hearts incline.

In the quiet, our truths we spin,
Whispered stories, felt deep within.
In the dance, new chapters begin,
Transcending silence, with a spin.

The Choreography of Chance Encounters

In life's grand stage, we often find,
Chance encounters, of the rarest kind.
With each step and turn, our paths entwined,
The choreography of fate, beautifully designed.

Strangers meet, in the dance of destiny,
Each step a note, in a symphony.
In the waltz of life, we move pensively,
Embracing moments, fleeting ceaselessly.

With a glance, a smile, the dance begins,
In the rhythm of chance, love often spins.
In unexpected moments, the future grins,
In chance encounters, new life begins.

Each movement tells, a story anew,
Of paths crossed, and friendships true.
In the dance of chance, we pursue,
Dreams and hopes, in vistas blue.

So we dance on, amidst life's grand parade,
In the choreography, fate has made.
With every encounter, a new foundation laid,
In the art of chance, our lives are swayed.

Revelations in the Art of Motion

In each step, a revelation,
In movement, life's true foundation.
The art of motion, a silent conversation,
With every gesture, a new realization.

Each jump, a leap towards the sky,
In the dance, our spirits fly.
Revelations born, as feet defy,
The gravity of the why.

In the twirls, secrets unbind,
Truths untangle, in the mind.
In the flow of motion, we find,
The mysteries of the kind.

Steps echo, in halls of thought,
Lessons in motion, subtly taught.
In the labyrinth of moves sought,
Revelations, in battles fought.

So we dance, in search of clue,
In motion, our souls renew.
With every step, our world view,
Transforms, in the dance's hue.

www.ingramcontent.com/pod-product-compliance
Lightning Source LLC
LaVergne TN
LVHW012244070526
838201LV00090B/112